Zen Brushpoems

Zen Brushpoems

Ray Grigg

CHARLES E. TUTTLE COMPANY, INC.
Boston • Rutland,Vermont • Tokyo

Published by the Charles E. Tuttle Company, Inc.
of Rutland, Vermont & Tokyo, Japan,
with editorial offices at 77 Central Street, Boston, Massachusetts 02109.

Library of Congress Cataloging-in-Publication Data
Grigg, Ray, 1938-
    Zen brushpoems / Ray Grigg
       p.   cm.
    ISBN 0-8048-1840-1
    1. Zen poetry, American. I. Title.
    PS3557.R48992Z44 1993
    811'.54—dc20
                                       92-46697
                                              CIP

First printing 1993
PRINTED IN THE UNITED STATES

To
Paul Reps

whose "poems before words"
I
read/saw
and was changed

Contents

Introduction

Writing and painting in China and Japan came from the same source. The present characters that constitute the written language of both cultures had a common beginning as Chinese pictograms, ancient and stylized picture-drawings that eventually abstracted into their existing forms. But this writing and painting never separated into two distinct expressions. Indeed, they have remained so closely related that even today the stroke components of writing continue to be used in painting. The Chinese painter uses the same brush techniques as the calligrapher and literally "writes a painting." So paintings in both China and Japan are quite naturally decorated, complemented, and completed with calligraphy.

This blending of words and pictures was also common in the West before the uniformity of the printing press displaced the handcrafting of words. In the age of illuminated manuscripts words were visually alive, actively in partnership with pictures to constitute the whole art of illumination. Before word-making and picture-making were separated by mechanical type in the late 15th century there was writing/painting. Words and pictures were related to each other by being crafted similarly. Each embellished and enhanced the other, gave energy and meaning to the other. Words and pictures belonged together because they were both visual metaphors for the same magic of representation, one depicting what the ear heard and the other what the eye saw. When the two appear together, the communicative effect of each is multiplied by the presence of the other.

Zen Brushpoems is an expression of this shared tradition of the East and West. By placing together the word and image, the brushpoems replicate the wholeness of reading/seeing that was once experienced in illuminated manuscripts and is still the key to appreciating Chinese and Japanese painting and calligraphy. For the present West, the brushpoems reconnect the phonetic metaphor of the written word with the visual metaphor of the painted image. Thus we are drawn closer to the mystery that is the source of metaphor but is not itself metaphor.

Words are metaphors. As metaphors they are a system of representation. Their shortcoming is that they impose their own form of abstraction and structure upon our understanding until their form becomes our understanding. The art of discourse is the shape of this metaphorical convention. Indeed, the more seriously we use language, the more it obscures the underlying mystery that it attempts to represent until, finally, we become so occupied with the system itself that we lose sight of what is not metaphorical. All philosophical problems are the invention of words.

The Japanese haiku is a model for acknowledging this shortcoming of words. The entire poem is constructed of a sparse seventeen syllables. Philosophy is abandoned. Explanation is eliminated. The discursive function of language is rejected. Discourse is minimized. Language is pared to critical essentials.

But what happens if the few stark syllables of the haiku are reduced to fewer than the formal seventeen? The words, with less and less context to support themselves, begin to collapse as a system. The form of understanding that we derive from discourse approaches crisis. The few words that remain lose their ability to support themselves as a meaningful structure. These remaining words need something else, a different metaphor to reconstitute and revitalize themselves. More words will not do. The palpable immediacy of the brushed image is perfect.

Of course, the brushed images are also metaphorical but they have a physicality that is more direct than words. They, too, represent but they are more fundamental, more grounded and primal than words. The brushed images add a new dimension of meaning to the words, expanding them out of the abstract circle of themselves.

Together the image and the words in each brushpoem complete each other. The brush's ink offers just the right physical presence to

x

give the words a weight and solidity, a depth and resonance, and, paradoxically, a curious lightness. The words begin to dance like the spontaneity of the brush, not depictive enough to be confining but suggestive enough to be expanding. Enlivened and stimulated by each other, the words and the brushed image have an effect that is comparable to the creative tension connecting the two verbal components of the traditional haiku. They both complement and juxtapose each other, balancing between the confinement of something said and the expansiveness of something suggested. Like the dynamics within the haiku, the words and the image in each brushpoem produce a creative tension in which the insight that is generated far exceeds what is capable by the individual components. The words give direction to the image, and the image gives resonance to the words. The whole effect of each brushpoem is created by the double impact of the written word and the painted image.

The impact that is generated by the creative tension between these two elements of metaphorical expression takes place in the space between them. This space is the genesis of our deepest understandings. It is an unconditional and unknowable source of insight. Like the space between two thoughts, it is experienced as emptiness.

All the words and images can be followed into emptiness. It is the reference for all knowing, the hidden source that teases us away from the confinement of every certainty. Emptiness is the mystery that lies outside the representational power of all words and images, the original mystery that is the source of metaphor but is itself not metaphor. It is, instead, an unformed certainty that lies outside conceptualization. Our task in *Zen Brushpoems* is, with a whole and balanced consciousness, to follow the words and images of the brushpoems into this emptiness.

We are, of course, the receptivity of this emptiness. But we rarely notice the emptiness itself, and we can never explain it because it is background to all thoughts, all expressions of thought, and all objects of thought. When we attempt to make emptiness an object of thought, it seems to become an elusive and undifferentiated negation. Not until mind is whole and balanced and still can emptiness be entered. Until then we are shadowed by a deep and profound sense of restless incompletion.

The words and images of *Zen Brushpoems* invite us to completion. They require that our thoughts become whole, balanced and still enough to enter emptiness. To fully engage the brushpoems we enter the words and images until we enter the emptiness that contains them. This emptiness is nothing, the condition of unrestrained receptivity. And thereby it becomes a fullness that is everything.

Zen Brushpoems

choose
your
own ...

laughter

3

waiting...
like moon
in water

sprout meeting sun

changing...

finding

6

just
enough...

everything

in emptiness
thoughts
echo
as ...

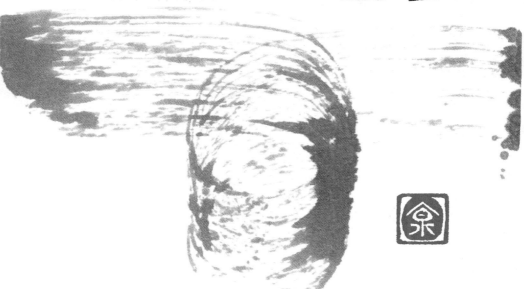

remembering

hold mirror
backwards...

to appear
by
disappearing

this
treefrog
croak . . .

for
me?

potato
eye...

like my
I

fern
unravelling...

fern
riddle

try
explaining
to
river

honourable
sage...

honourable
fool

with eyes
listening ...

bluebells
ring

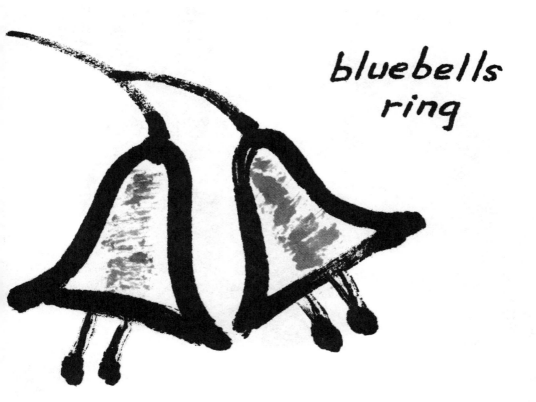

accounting
for every...

stoneshape

wave and sea . . .

divided only by
thoughts

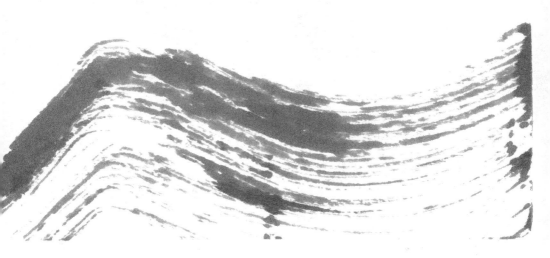

sides...

of
argument

how can
this
wisp
of
self...

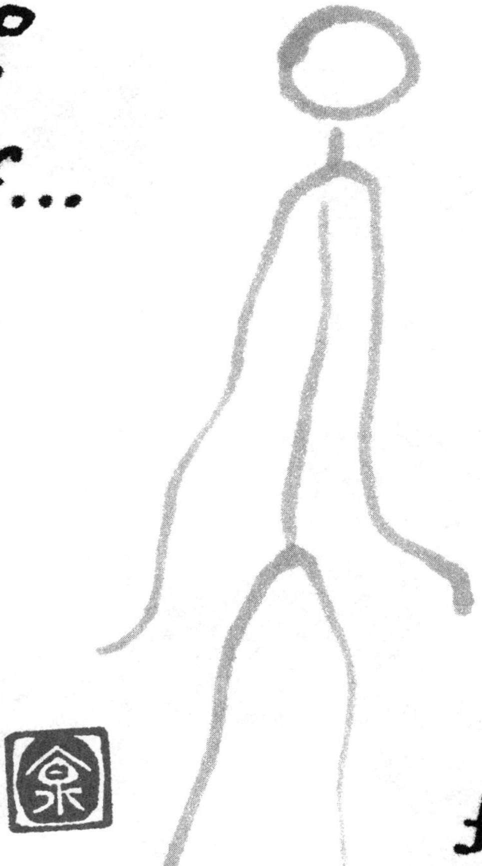

feel
so
heavy

thank...

you

me

us

20

between
you
and
me...

not
even
a
sound

emptiness...
from
filled
bowl

we
two...

inwardly
downwardly
togethering

23

like
splitting
stones ...

with
feathers

how to change these stone bones...

into a softer me?

25

short
staff...

for
beating
out
ego

belly thinking...
belly laughing

Pah!
Three times called
and still...

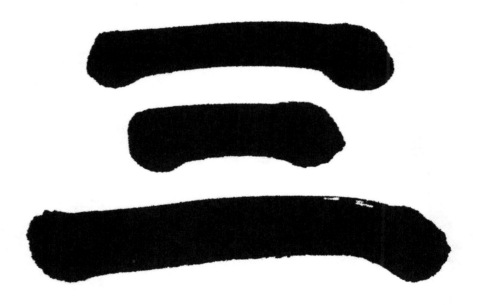

I don't
answer
myself

sky
history...

of
leaf

doing
as if
waiting...

waiting
as if
doing

30

think...
like
sky

flowering . . .

explaining
flower

eye
echo...

eye
echo

square thought
thinking ...

round
me

gently

downwardly

softening

sprouting

36

under covers...
toes touching
goodnight

whole
self...

no
self

easy
starting ...

easy
stopping

water...

minded

no
longer   pretending...

to be
me

music...
for deaf
eyes

seeking
light
in the
centre

of
darkness

river flowing
through...

 emptiness
in river

never
quite ...

who I
think
I am

raindrops ...
wetting
lake

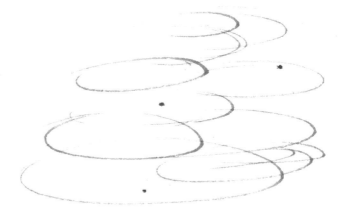

smilingly
begin ...

everywhere
at once

easy up...

easy down...

balancing

tree turning whole world...

into tree

downwardly

following

stone
breathing
easily...

with
me

51

fingertipsing...

our
yes

thoughtlessly...

changing
mind

receiving honour...

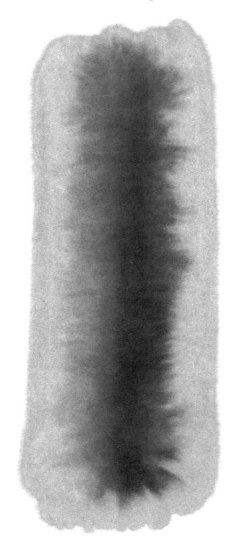

indifferently

including ...

excluded

leaves
shadow-dancing...

just
for
us

head bone...

held up
by

leg
bone

just
you...
me...

should
be
easy

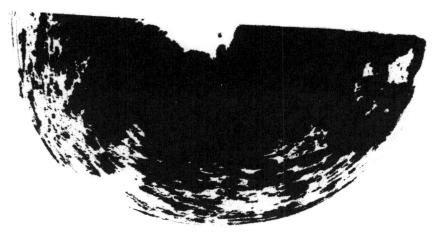

sun
flowering...

flower
sunning

always
enough...

emptiness

let
us
go

our
separate
ways...

together

indifferent
to...

differences

with two-eyed
          glasses...

see with
   one eye

indiscriminate
cherry ...

offering
itself
even to
crows

64

after
so many
years

these
fingertips...

still
touch

stringlessly
flying . . .

kite
thoughts

butterfly's
   window
     dilemma . . .

                    mine
                    too

stone
erodes...

before
water

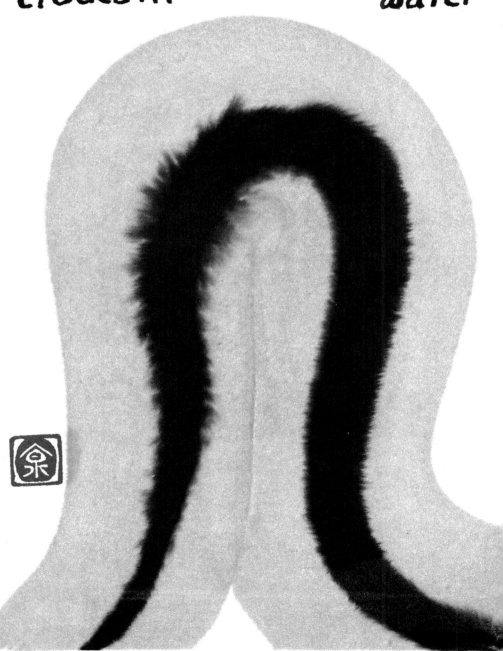

with
  yes eye...

listen

finally
only...

my
own
way

deep
in these stone
bones...

something
unknowable
knows

tree - top ...
growing
mountain
higher

how to
know...

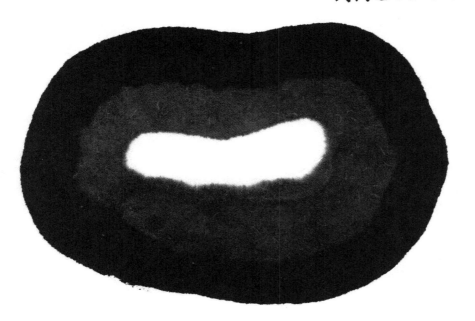

inside of
stone

beginning
and
end

same
and different

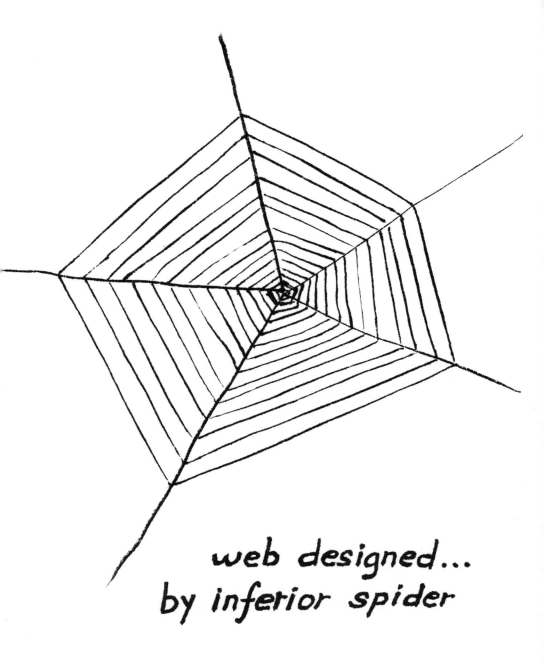

web designed...
by inferior spider

each
leaf...

falls
differently

somehow
becoming...

who I always was

carefully
attending to . . .

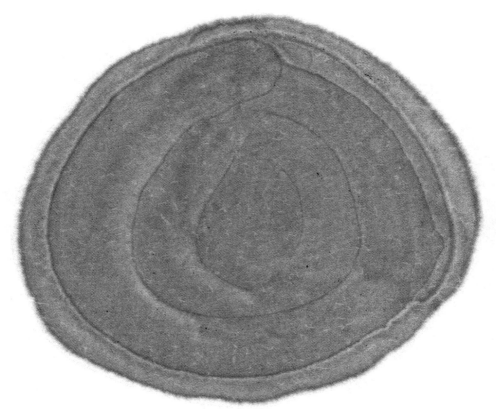

leaving
undone

pretending ...

not
to
know

like
flower...

smiling
yes

silence...

always
in
tune

once each
year...

a special spring

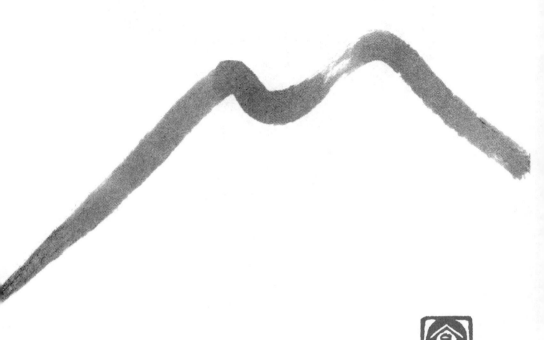

move pebble ...
and whole
distant mountain
shudders

big
me...

merely on
rice paper

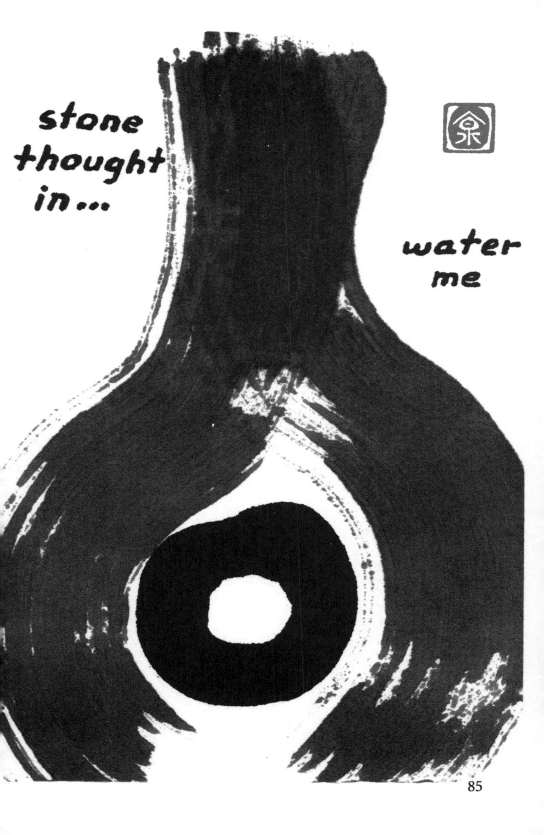

stone
thought
in...

water
me

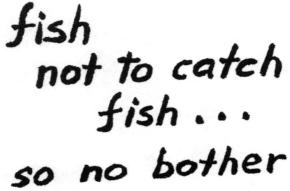

fish
not to catch
fish . . .
so no bother

let
scissors
choose
flower...

and
moment

87

sky
house

world
me ...

righting
world

bowl
full
of...

empty
sky

waxing and
waning...

this
bittersweet

lollipop
moon

small space...
big enough for
everything

does
bright
moonlight

disturb
flowers

like seeing
      tree...

enter
   stone

tickle
of...

smile
smiling

sinking
into ...

each
other

sea
and
sky...

separated
only by
remembering

now...

no trace
of mistake

out...

coming

who are we...

but
shadows

pretending
to
be

where
in me
are...

ancient
teachings

perhaps . . .

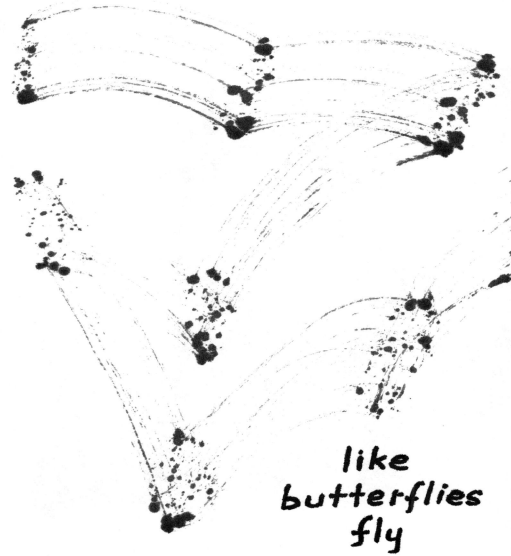

like
butterflies
fly